CLOISTER

BOOKS

Cloister Books are inspired by the monastic custom of walking slowly and reading or meditating in the monastery cloister, a place of silence, centering, and calm. Within these pages you will find a similar space in which to pray and reflect on the presence of God.

Praying the Hours

Praying
the
Hours

Suzanne Guthrie

COWLEY PUBLICATIONS
Cambridge · Boston
Massachusetts

Library of Congress Cataloging-in-Publication Data:
    Guthrie, Suzanne, 1951–
    Praying the hours / Suzanne Guthrie.
    p. cm.
    ISBN:1-56101-177-0 (alk. paper)
    1. Meditations. I. Title.
BV4832.2 .G86 2000
242—dc21
Scripture quotations are from the *New Revised Standard
Version of the Bible,* © 1989 by the Division of Christian
Education of the National Council of the Churches of Christ
in the USA. Used by permission. All rights reserved.

Cynthia Shattuck: editor; Annie Kammerer, copyeditor
Cover and interior design by Vicki Black
Cover photograph: "Madonna lily, the Cuxa Cloister Garth
Garden, Manhattan, New York," © 1990 Sam Abell

This book was printed by Versa Press in the United States of
America on recycled, acid-free paper.

Cowley Publications
28 Temple Place • *Boston, Massachusetts 02111*
800-225-1534 • *www.cowley.org*

To Bill Consiglio,
with whom I live in sacred time and place

Processu vero conversationis et fidei,
dilato corde inenarrabili dilectionis dulcedine
curritur via mandatorum Dei.
(Prologus:49, Regula Sancti Benedicti*)*

Table of Contents

II. *Praying in Time*

Acknowledgments

The meditations in this book have been presented as retreat material at Holy Cross Monastery in West Park, The Community of the Holy Spirit in Manhattan, Yale Divinity School in New Haven, and the Benedictine Experience at the Bishop's Ranch in Healdsburg, California.

I wish to thank Robert Sevensky OHC, Jean Campbell OSH, and Randy Horton, Hermit, for advice and the loan of books. I thank the Camaldolese Benedictines for time at the hermitage and use of their monastic library, especially Robert Hale OSB Cam., Cyprian Consiglio OSB Cam., and Bernard Massicotte OSB Cam. for materials I would not have been able to find or use without their help.

Thank you, Linda Duval, Anne Kitch, Kathy Still, and especially Linda Fite and Sister Élise CHS who read and corrected the manuscript. Thank you, Bill, willing to translate Latin to English at any holy or unholy hour of the day or night.

Thank you, brothers at Holy Cross Monastery, with whom I worship, and sisters of The Community of the Holy Spirit, who offer me hospitality and spiritual direction.

I thank all my brothers and sisters in monastic life who share stories, time, humor, and the joys and sorrows of life with me.

I also thank the always supportive and patient Cynthia Shattuck and the staff at Cowley Publications.

Prologue

Rejoice always, pray without ceasing, give
thanks in all circumstances; for this is the
will of God in Christ Jesus for you.

1 Thessalonians 5:16-18

When I was eleven years old I was given my own copy of *The Book of Common Prayer*. The white leather prayer book fit perfectly in my hands, and my name was embossed in gold on the cover. I loved my prayer book, and kept it on the nightstand. I prayed every day on my knees next to my bed. Saying the beautiful prayers made me happy, and I sensed the sacred phrases shaping my unformed soul.

At the age of twenty-two I read *The Autobiography of St. Teresa of Avila,* Teresa's sixteenth-century account of an adventurous journey of prayer. Her humor, integrity, and richness of soul inspired me to renew my own life of prayer. I sought out spiritual direction and began to study the writings of Teresa of Avila, John of the Cross, and other Christian mystics. That same year I also began theological studies at a Roman Catholic seminary, taking advantage of the open, ecumenical spirit of the post-Vatican II church. Most of my classmates and friends were in religious orders and we often talked about prayer. Although I began my studies by concentrating in the Bible, I found myself drawn more and more to spirituality, prayer, and Christian mysticism.

Prologue

So I have prayed, worshiped, and studied in monastic houses of different kinds the whole of my adult life. Since the morning and evening worship services of *The Book of Common Prayer* are based on the sevenfold offices of ancient monastic prayer, monastic worship offered a spiritual continuity I have taken for granted all these years, even as a married woman with four children. Praying the same prayers I loved as a child in my house with monks and nuns in *their* houses seemed natural—prayers as familiar as the tissue-thin pages of the little white prayer book that shaped my soul. The daily rhythms of monastic prayer became a part of my own conscious habit of prayer.

The first thing I ever learned about praying was the importance of finding a certain time and a specific place for prayer. Your soul then becomes alert in anticipation, just as your stomach does if you eat at noon every day. Praying in a certain time and place establishes a habit of prayer at the heart of your day and in your surroundings, or, as my friend Sister Élise describes it, "a way the Holy Spirit may find you ready every day."

Seven times a day do I praise you (Psalm 119:164). Knowing full well that seven is a mystical number meaning "at all times," St. Benedict prepared seven prayer offices for his monks to say during waking hours. The monks were to drop whatever they were doing at the sound of the bell and go with haste to the chapel to pray Matins, Lauds, Terce, Sext, None, Vespers, and Compline. But as later Benedictine commentators would affirm, the seven times were an "outline" of prayer, "pillars of a bridge thrown across the stream of time."

Today traditional monks and nuns may also file into the chapel several times a day for the prayer offices, but the offices they recite simply connect the "between time" by means of mutual community prayer. What about the rest of time? And what about those of us who do not live with others who pray habitually through the day? How can we "rejoice always," as St. Paul tells us, and give thanks in all circumstances?

For me, being mindful of the presence of God in daily life requires devotional practices that can be folded into the times of a hectic day and accompany me throughout my daily travels. Eating, sleeping, and even dusting the house have to lift my heart to God. The Holy Spirit must find me not only at home but at work, running errands, and in all the settings of my erratic schedule.

While most of us cannot stop work to say a prayer office seven times a day, at least thinking about the holy hours can provide a method for remembering the presence of God in daily life. The ancient sevenfold pattern of monastic prayer provides a framework for praying continually. If I begin by remembering and praising God seven times a day, perhaps seven will break through and become seven mystically. Then I will pray at all times and in all circumstances. My own tradition gives me those pillars of a bridge of prayer arching through the hours of my waking and my sleeping.

The written prayers of our liturgical tradition offer us a textbook for prayer in time. But we are invited to do more than merely recite the words: they prepare us for what we will find beyond and behind the prayers themselves. A monk I know once told me about a woman who complained that she had "run out of prayers to say." He responded, "Ah, good! Prayer is what happens when you run out of words."

Moving to a new house last year also gave me an opportunity to think about praying—praying not only in time, but in space, and the need to pray in familiar places every day. Stability of place is as important for prayer as having regular times in which to do it. So this book of meditations is a way of sharing with you my own efforts to deepen and enlarge my prayer by sanctifying both space and time in new surroundings and under all circumstances.

I

Praying in Place

one

Moving

A New House

LORD, who may dwell in your tabernacle?
who may abide upon your holy hill?

Psalm 15:1

Every time I have ever moved, I have had to learn to pray all over again. This is not because my new surroundings are a distraction, but rather that my prayer becomes so much a part of the scents and sounds and geography around me that I must learn my new environment before I pray. Wherever I am, I have to learn to listen, to see, and to wait.

Imagine a child finding his mother again after he is born: tasting her not in the amniotic salt of womb water but in the honey of her milk, and hearing her not in her nearby heartbeat, but in the clear sounds of her laughter and speaking and singing. Or imagine him trying to find her in the night, rooting through blanket folds guided by the combined scents of her breath, her hands, her clothing, and the lingering touch of lavender. Imagine him learning to call her to himself with his own new voice.

When I move to a new house, I also experience the initial discomfort of learning to hear the divine voice behind unfamiliar sounds, to recognize again the intimacy of God behind new scents, to perceive divine light behind the shifting sunlight throughout the house by day. I explore my home's darkness and lean toward the warmth of familiar love waiting for me behind the deepest part of the night.

One day, before the sale of this new house is final, I investigate the backyard while I wait for the realtor. The cellar door is open and I make my way through the dark basement and up the stairs to the kitchen. I visit all the empty rooms, praying as I go, asking blessings upon this house and the life we will live here, trying to perceive a holy presence in this new place. The house is so dirty, and so in need of repair! It smells like the succession of tenants who, neighbors tell me later, seemed to revolve in and out every few months. And dogs. Hairs, long and black, in nests where a large dog curled up to sleep. Dirt. Dust. This is difficult prayer. Even the short prayer that pierces heaven falls back into my heart with a thud.

Finally I hear footsteps downstairs and interrupt my reverie, bounding down to greet the realtor coming through the front door—only to find the house still empty. It is just the sound of the house itself, this old creaky house on its handmade foundation of rocks, the aged wood sighing from eighty years of footsteps.

There is so much to do here! How long will it take to make this home? The floors are full of stains and dirt that have worn into the wood, and the kitchen linoleum erupts in bubbles and sinks in caves from years of water leaking from behind the cabinets. We have inherited yellowed walls, cracked tiles, ugly wallpaper of blue roses interrupted with brown seams. At least it is a sunny house. I try to imagine lace curtains, bookcases, plants. White walls reflecting sunshine.

"You won't have to worry about radon," remarks the inspector. "The house has...um... excellent ventilation."

As discouraged as I am, my husband ventures into the project with enthusiasm for all the endless handyman chores to do. The attic is open to the outside in the eaves, the drainpipes and gutters hang off the house, spindles are missing on the porch. Don't lean against that porch rail! Hanging only from a large misplaced nail, it is about to tumble into the street. The small yard is overgrown with brush and weeds; sumac and catalpa and maple saplings need cutting, sawing, and hauling. Lady, my small Welsh corgi who is used to endless acres of farmland and woods, will have to be fenced in.

"What about those blue roses?"

"I don't do wallpaper," smiles my husband.

Prevenient grace. I learned that word once. It is the kind of grace that goes before you to prepare a place for you. It is grace that tabernacles beneath the fire and cloud bidding you follow from place to place, anticipating your hesitation, your desire, your reluctance. The grace you find when you get there. The grace of your mother's arms after you are born. The grace that already knows that, eventually, you will come no matter how cranky you are about it.

Grace invites us toward sanctification of our souls. The ancient eastern church overcomes our instinctive fear of hubris and invites us to "deification," to grow more and more into the image and likeness of God, that most undeserved gift. Drawn toward grace we are given power to become children of God. But we have to want it. And trust it.

Trusting in God, however reluctantly, is a good spiritual exercise. Monks and nuns test themselves through the vow of obedience.

Obedience teaches anticipation of God's grace in any situation: it is the spiritual practice of faithfulness, of simply playing in prevenient grace. Therefore any move or undesired change can be used as a spiritual exercise—the harder the move, the better the exercise! That is what I tell myself, anyway.

14

Before this move, my soul's home was the view from our farmhouse, with the Rondout Valley below and the lower Catskill Mountains opposite: High Point, Slide, Mombaccus. This was my prayer for seven years, an easy prayer, because the first thing I saw in the morning was the grandeur of space and primitive beauty as if the earth had been created moments ago. Seeing Adam and Eve walking out from beneath the catalpa tree would not have surprised me. My soul was shaped by this expanse of sight—the solitude, the silence, enclosed by forest and rock cliffs. I had hoped to spend the rest of my life in that house. But how many other hermit souls have sucked in their breath obediently and lived and worked in cities until their apostolic duties were complete?

Moving

It simply is not practical to live on a mountain at this time in my life. My son's school is now in Poughkeepsie, a city that is some distance away, and my own work takes me into town and to New York City, where I commute by train to be among people. Silence and solitude will have to wait for some other season. But I do not have to be cheerful about it.

We rent a truck and move over a weekend. The biggest job is moving my library. I had packed my books into computer paper boxes over a course of many weeks—one carefully arranged box at a time. I labeled each one in case I needed something, which I often did, moving this or that box to dig for a quotation or a line or to look up the meaning of some scripture passage. I took access to my books for granted during the sad summer before we moved—the time of meeting the demands of the buyer and bringing the old farmhouse up to the unrealistic expectations of a city dweller and first-time homeowner. This summer of scouting out the new territory, grieving over the old territory, my four children coming and going, beginning a new job, and the complex process of selling and buying a house with lawyers mixing up dates and losing papers and changing closing times was a disconcerting, disorienting time. But at least I could find a book when I needed it.

A few days after we move our boxes and furniture, still sleeping as many nights as possible at the farmhouse, I come to the front door of the new house and look through the window into the living room. There are all those boxes of books, neatly stacked. I can read the magic marker labels: Biblical Ref., Judaica, Carmelite Studies, Desert/Anchorites, Merton, Holocaust Lit., Benedictine Monastic Lit., Islam, Children's Spirituality Stuff.

Prevenient grace! I wish I were not so shallow and so small a soul that I should need a huge pile of books—like the proverbial elephant in the living room—to remind me of grace! How many boxes of books? At least thirty. Not counting the encyclopedias we carried in shopping bags. Dog-eared, worn, underlined, marked up and notched with paperclips for easy reference for teaching or preaching, chewed in some cases by children or puppies, these books have been prayer and presence in all sorts and conditions of my soul, in all kinds of times. These saints and sinners, men and women, holy hasids and holy idiots have lived with me and accompanied me in tragedy as well as in peace. These pages, some falling apart from the sheer delight of reading them again and again, remind me of my hidden hours. Books once concealed in the secret room under the stairs, or behind the toilet rolls in the bathroom cabinet. Here are the friends that live across time, now in full view, dominating my living room. Hail, hail, the gang's all here!

Suddenly I feel a shift in my attitude, if not my very soul. I feel like St. Teresa bringing the reserved sacrament into a new convent. Now I scrub and clean with vigor, washing each shelf and closet in this house with orange-scented Citrasolv, sweeping around those boxes again and again to rid the house of foreign dog hair. From now on the dog hair in our house will be corgi red and white! The dust will be our dust. I will make this new place a sacred place. A place of prayer. I will make it home.

Lord Jesus Christ, make this a temple of your presence and a house of prayer. Be always near us when we seek you in this place. Draw us to you, when we come alone and when we come with others, to find comfort and wisdom, to be supported and strengthened, to rejoice and give thanks. May it be here, Lord Christ, that we are made one with you and with one another, so that our lives are sustained and sanctified for your service.

prayer for the consecration of a church,
BCP 568

18

two

Sensing

Sounds and Scents

And the Word became flesh
and lived among us.

John 1:14

O nce I felt so sudden and strong a presence of the divine that I fell prostrate in front of the washing machine. I finally picked myself up off the floor and hung my load of clean, wet diapers across the clothesline, laughing the whole time. What else is there to do but laugh when you have just been struck dumb before God in the laundry room?

What I remember of this sacred moment twenty-five years later comes from my senses and my interpretation of my senses. I do not remember what God was like at all, but I somehow knew divine presence had broken upon me, and consequently I was overwhelmingly awed. I remember the sun-drenched diapers on the line and, most of all, how illogical and deeply funny I thought the experience was even moments after it happened.

Moving to a new living space is such a disruption of the senses that it is initially bad for prayer, although ultimately good. A slight panic interrupts my habit of morning praise as I rummage around for the coffee grinder in this unfamiliar kitchen—but on the other hand its unfamiliarity heightens my senses, as if I am traveling in a foreign country where each unique scent or sound, shape, texture, or color lends clarity to my memory later on.

What is that horrible acrid smell that pervades everything, especially when it is damp outside? Eventually Bill and I realize that the smell comes from scab-like black marks on the maple leaves. Across the street the maple trees look dead; ours looks merely sick. The black stuff falls to the ground, clings to my shoes, comes with me into the car and into the house. Residue of the blight drips onto the desktop that I am working on outside made from an old door. The stench lives with me for weeks, painted into my desk.

Other scents define the neighborhood. Truckloads of apples sit outside at the juice company on the next block. Mountains of apples left overnight or for days perfume the air with the sweetness of mulled cider. I smell marinara sauce from three pizza kitchens and several Italian restaurants within an easy walk, and I am suddenly hungry for anchovies and capers, delicate pasta, clam sauce . . . and apple pie.

I cannot imagine ever getting used to the screech of highway traffic. If someone from long ago should suddenly walk into our neighborhood, he would go mad from the sound. The highway echoes under the bridge, amplifying the rumbling weight of trucks that sound like imperial enemy TIE fighters from the *Star Wars* movies. And as my son Patrick observes, it smells horribly of car exhaust right under the highway where we walk into the center of town. Children playing, doors slamming; people arguing, raking, shoveling, and hammering; lawnmowers rumbling, basketballs pounding the concrete. I had forgotten how to live with neighborhood sounds.

These aural boundaries complicate my dog Lady's sense of duty. Initially the neighborhood comings and goings drive her crazy. Keenly sensitive, her wide boundaries at the farmhouse required her to protect us only from deer grazing under our apple trees or in the meadow below, and occasionally she alerted us to an errant direction of the wind. She knew every car going up or down the hill. So to restrict her space and expect her to guard us from all the people on this street, including the mailman (who comes right up on our porch!) and all the dogs, cats, and squirrels—as well as every car, bicycle, Rollerblade, basketball, and skateboard—is a lot to ask of a cow-herding dog fiercely devoted to me, her lone cow.

One night I am asleep in the front room with Lady curled at my feet. Below, in the yard of the house next door, a neighbor ties his two big dogs to a tree. Lady barks. Once. I comfort and calm her, assuring her that everything is fine despite the disturbing fact that our neighbor's yard is right beneath our window, and there are two big dogs right there. But her bark sets the two off until a police cruiser pulls up, lights flashing. The officer knocks next door until the neighbor answers. "Look, Lady!" I whisper. "You got those two big dogs in trouble!" We watch from the upstairs darkness, and to my relief, Lady does not bark at the officer. Another neighbor had called the police. Not long after this, we put a fence around our lot, and Lady learns that this will be her new boundary.

Outside in the garden back at the farmhouse, a chipmunk once escaped from our cat and ran right up the inside of my blue jeans. I screamed as loud as I ever have in my life, while the animal ran around in a panic inside my pants and up my blouse and back down the inside of my other pant leg. Not one neighbor heard me. Here, Lady barks once from inside the house and the police come for the neighbor's dogs. I learn that the police make fun of the guy across the street for his frequent calls regarding dogs. The farm was a good place for a hermit. Town is a good place for a gossip.

Now we know the beep! beep! of the car horn each morning at ten of nine in front of the house that used to be a florist. We know the flash of headlights and the motor starting under our window on the other side, when our neighbor leaves to drive his sanitation truck every morning at a quarter past three. We know the warming up sound of the half-sized bus across the street and the rumble of a heating fuel truck bumping down the little rise where it is parked one house over. We know the step of Ron, our mailman, although Lady still barks happily when he comes up onto the porch. Both Lady and I now know the names and voices of all the children on the block. But I am still not used to the highway.

My prayer molds itself to these boundaries drawn by my senses. This new house is now my sanctuary, the place from which I pray and go into the world to work. Every smell, sound, and sight

24

connects me to my place and my time. In prayer I do not want to take my senses for granted, but neither do I want to escape them. We are created in such a way that we interpret through our senses as well as our intellect—sight, sound, smell, touch, and taste have ensured our survival as human beings since before we walked upright. And perhaps our senses are made for transcendence.

Through my senses, I learned to pray. I taught myself to meditate by listening—to music, to people talking—and over time I taught myself to find a quiet place to listen so deeply I could hear my breathing, and then my heart. Finally, I learned to hear beyond my senses.

Christians sometimes think you need to conquer the senses in order to pray, but it is far more efficient to first give the body the attention it begs for and deserves. St. Teresa of Avila, writing centuries ago on the art of prayer, said that it was important to be comfortable when you pray. Who can concentrate on prayer while the knees complain bitterly of the hard, cold floor? Instead, she advised, attend to the senses and acknowledge the body, preparing yourself for the reverence for which you were created.

Rather than providing an escape from reality, praying heightens our awareness. God uses our senses; our impressions fold into prayer like handfuls of flour kneaded into dough. The senses become the substance within which rises a sense of the sacred.

After all, the Word became flesh—and sight and sound and touch. And before the Word died on the cross, he probably suffered all those small assaults upon his senses: toothaches, swollen feet, skin rashes, head colds, low blood sugar, insomnia from time to time. Jesus himself was sense, dwelling in time and place.

> O God, *who wonderfully created, and yet more wonderfully restored, the dignity of human nature: Grant that we may share the divine life of him who humbled himself to share our humanity, your Son Jesus Christ; who lives and reigns with you, in the unity of the Holy Spirit, one God, for ever and ever. Amen.*

collect of the Incarnation, BCP 252

three

Censing

Dust and Incense

The LORD God formed man from the dust of the ground, and breathed into his nostrils the breath of life; and the man became a living being.

Genesis 2:7

B efore we came here I had forgotten how dust travels right through windows. It has been a long time since I lived in a city or town, where cars stir up the dirt on the street and the silt of city pollution rains continually into living space regardless of roof and walls. In this house we have forced hot air heat, which takes the dusty air from the house, sucks it up through fat silver ducts snaking through the basement into the furnace, and, despite the workings of a series of filters, recycles the dust right back in again.

We notice the film of dust most readily on the white tile in the bathroom. And on the tops of books. What is this doing to my computer? Our lungs? Our skin? We are a feast for a whole cosmos of dust mites who claim they were here first. We have to dust with damp rags and wet the floors where we would ordinarily just sweep. Day and night we run a portable humidifier that pours gallons of water into the air to help balance the dry atmosphere.

So the battle against dirt and dust begins in the space where we live and move and have our being. The rhythm of life in this space will require a rigorous cycle of cleaning and washing, purgation and ablution. When the dog sneezes, I know there is danger at knee level. Lady is the warning canary of the dusty canyons between furniture legs. Warning, Mistress! The dust is rising as you walk by! See it gathering with tufts of my white fur at the base of the piano, around the legs of the dining table. . . . Ah-choo!

In the words of Psalm 119, *My soul cleaves to the dust; give me life according to your word* (v. 25). My soul cleaves to the dust from which I am made. But I also lean into the life that breathes from the breath of God. We are dust balls ourselves, yet capable of singing at our graves. In the burial office we say:

> We are mortal, formed of the earth, and to earth shall we return. For so did you ordain when you created me, saying, "You are dust, and to dust you shall return." All of us go down to the dust; yet even at the grave we make our song: Alleluia, alleluia, alleluia. (BCP 499)

I once asked a doctor why he chose medicine as a profession. We were sitting alone together on a ski lift, traveling up a mountain as the earth seemed to fall from beneath us again and again. The giant mountains diminished as time passed, as the air thinned, here above the clouds. "I went into medicine because I hated and feared death," he replied. After a time he added, "But even in medicine I find there is little I can do to fight the enemy after all." Suddenly the frozen earth came up to meet us, the safety bar flew open, and we quickly slipped off the chair and down the chute. The doctor skied at a death-defying pace down the mountain, while I, somewhat afraid of the adventure before me, stayed a while to look at the view and whisper the *Gloria in excelsis Deo* under my breath before easing my way down the mountain.

Because I am earthbound and made of dust, I am deathbound and will return to dust. My time will end in dying, at some time I cannot predict, later or sooner, or even sooner than that. What makes me think that there is more than dust, or that the dust is somehow magical, is that I can stand, freezing, at the top of a mountain, and sing the *Gloria* under my breath. *Let everything that has breath praise the Lord.* I am a dust ball that sings. The extravagance of that!

Censing

One of my favorite books as a child was *Rebecca of Sunnybrook Farm* by Kate Douglas Wiggin. The Simpson family, who lived near Rebecca's aunts, were extremely poor and the father was a ne'er-do-well. The Simpson children sold cakes of soap, not for money but for a premium—the gift the soap company sent with the sale of a certain number of boxes. Simply for the adventure of it, Rebecca was wildly successful in selling an abundance of soap on behalf of the Simpsons. The premium arrived in time for Thanksgiving: it was a kerosene banquet lamp with a red crepe shade. The aunts observed that since the Simpsons did not even have enough food for Thanksgiving dinner, it was ridiculous for them to own an ostentatious lamp that did the poor family little good. To Rebecca, however, the lamp gave the hungry family a sense of warmth and glow and comfort that was a feast in itself. Like Mary of Bethany anointing Jesus with her expensive jar of ointment over Judas's reasonable objections, sometimes pure extravagance is the best thing.

For the same reason, if I am going to go to all the trouble of cleaning my house and fighting the incessant showers of dust and dirt, I am going to take one extra step after cleaning, and purify the house with incense. I have a bowl of stones from the shore of the Hudson River upon which I place a charcoal and incense I buy from the monastery.

I light the charcoal outside and pour the incense on the coal before going back in to pray my way silently through each room. I pray for each person who inhabits the house and anyone who finds rest or comfort here as guest or neighbor. I pray in every corner, at each turn and threshold, over places to rest and chairs to study in, and at all the functional places: the sink, the table, the toilet, the beds, the work areas, the piano, the bookcases, the attic. I pray that in each place we will fulfill the particular duty given by God.

The use of incense is primitive, a means of purification and sanctification long ago, even before written history. For me, incense evokes Sunday mornings, the scent sticking to our coats and clothes throughout the day, giving us an aura of sanctity, blessedness, church, community, purification. And extravagance. Incense is expensive.

Censing

The scent of incense in my house reminds me that my home is a sanctuary and a place of prayer. Worship takes place in the midst of mundane tasks, in the little dramas of human relationship that play out in a family. When I burn incense I offer my life-breath back to God, the bad and the good: the breath in words I wish I had not said, and the breath that turns to song, and the unconscious breathing that marks my time between earth to earth, ashes to ashes, and dust to dust.

We may be earth dust, but we are also star dust. Our elements consist of dust before time. We may carry the seeds of death in our flesh and bones, but deeper still we carry the shards of eternal life behind the universe. Time creates the illusion of transience. Patrick, rag in hand and working his way down the wooden banister, asks, "Where does all this dust come from? What is dust, anyway?"

Dust is the refuse of the universe. Refuse until it is shaken out of broom and dust rag over the compost heap, mingling with rich garden loam and, after a time, spread over new seedlings. Reborn, dust soaks into the very life of the herb garden—basil in my sandwich, parsley in the soup, and lavender blossoms that provide a feast for bees before they are harvested for my linen chest to freshen the scent of sheets. Dust is easy to explain, because I am dust. Dust is matter recycled through time. But what is time?

To this question even the typically verbose St. Augustine replies, "What, then, is time? I know well enough what it is, provided that nobody asks me; but if I am asked what it is and try to explain, I am baffled." But he also says in his *Confessions* that time is his giving himself back to God: "You made all time; you are before all time; and the time, if such we may call it, when there was no time was not time at all."

According to my dictionary, time is "the period between two events or during which something exists, happens, or acts; a measured or measurable interval." Time is how and when the dust settles. A more poetic encyclopedia says that while space is the dimension of movement, time is the dimension of becoming.

The dimension of movement is how we become in time. Even in repose, we are in perpetual movement as we breathe and our hearts beat and our blood courses through our bodies and the synapses in our brains continually charge with the electric impulses of our thoughts and dreams. And even after we die our bodies are dust, dust that moves and floats and lands on banisters to be mopped up and shaken outside.

But when I dance, I use time to defy gravity and kick up the dust that settles beneath my feet. I fill my house with music and dance my way round about, Lady barking at my heels. I dance for God and for the sheer fun of it. I dance my prayer and stretch the movement of my being beyond whatever I thought possible, strengthening my muscles, using gravity to push myself closer to heaven, above the dust, to mingle with incense rising to the sphere of the Most High.

The prophet Isaiah once saw the incense offering in the temple mingle with the smoky train of God's mantle:

> I saw the Lord sitting on a throne, high and lofty; and the hem of his robe filled the temple.... The pivots on the thresholds shook at the voices of those who called, and the house filled with smoke. (Isaiah 6:1, 4)

Perhaps the incense offering of my soul mingles somehow with the cloud of Presence, my offering indistinguishable from the veil that protects my senses from the presence of God. I may be dust, O Blessed, Holy One, but I know I am your dust!

36

Almighty and everlasting God, you made the universe with all its marvelous order, its atoms, worlds, and galaxies, and the infinite complexity of living creatures: Grant that, as we probe the mysteries of your creation, we may come to know you more truly, and more surely fulfill our role in your eternal purpose; in the name of Jesus Christ our Lord. Amen.

prayer for knowledge of God's creation,
BCP 827

four

Gardening

Once and Future Figs

My beloved speaks and says to me:
"Arise, my love, my fair one,
    and come away;
for now the winter is past,
    the rain is over and gone.
The flowers appear on the earth;
    the time of singing has come,
and the voice of the turtledove

is heard in our land.
The fig tree puts forth its figs,
  and the vines are in blossom;
  they give forth fragrance."

The Song of Solomon 2:10-13

38

U ncle Andrew Consiglio gave us a fig tree for our new house. Figs do not winter in the Hudson Valley, so around here you have to plant a big tub in the ground outside and the fig lives there all summer. Come winter you dig up the tub, and the tree goes into the basement. Our neighbor Joseph's fig tree is so big he can no longer get it into the basement, but builds a shed around it every winter.

Our fig has already sent out long green shoots with double-thumbed, mitten-like leaves suddenly crowding outward from its tender trunk. Will it give fruit this coming summer? Will we have our own soft, sensual figs, blood-red on the inside with seeds and sweet sticky pulp? Already we have lettuce, spinach, and broccoli raab to eat and

to give away, strawberries ripening, and herbs—
thyme, parsley, lemon balm, chamomile, winter
savory, basil, sage, rosemary, and chives—crowding each other in raised wooden beds. A new stem
of Concord grape vine twines up the arbor Bill
built against the house behind the kitchen garden;
we measure it every day simply to marvel at its
rapid growth.

When we moved, Bill set to work immediately
to transform this ugly city lot into a small paradise. He rented a backhoe to dig post holes for
the fence and found huge rocks beneath the soil
that had been part of an old stone wall. With two
truckloads of topsoil and compost, he created a
long berm, an earthen rise, to give the landscape
some visual interest, and then took all the
exposed rocks and made two small stone walls
against it. Next he gathered even more rocks to
create a waterfall trickling into a little pond. He
made a simple cement brick patio and sowed
seeds for a deep green lawn, then dug up ferns
from the forest behind our old house and trans-
planted them into our shady back border. He
surrounded the side yard with a picket fence
that the neighborhood children painted white

one morning in exchange for hot dogs and ice cream sundaes. Finally, he built a beautiful curved arbor for a creamy autumn clematis and a white climbing rose.

When the nurseries began divesting themselves of plants in the late fall, I took advantage of every clearance sale possible and filled the empty spaces around the edges of the yard with shrubs, perennials, and bulbs. The side yard with the picket fence is now my cottage garden, a shameless riot of eccentric fancy. Plants are grouped by color, with blues, reds, yellows—and even black hollyhocks and pansies. I grow wildflowers, blossoms that are hospitable to bees and butterflies, Chinese lanterns, sea holly, giant sunflowers, and a pumpkin vine. Wild and overcrowded, the cottage garden tames my messy eclecticism within a discrete circle inside a picket fence, centered by a birdbath. Pots of geraniums help secure the watering hose along the path.

You reach the backyard of our house through the cottage garden and rose bower. I had long dreamed of creating a white garden in the backyard, inventing and reimagining with soft pencil on pages of graph paper, surrounded by garden books and carefully collected magazine articles. I would dream my ideal garden every winter, usually huddled near the wood stove in the farmhouse under a quilt on the old couch, wearing boots and kerchief and layers of sweaters, trying to keep warm and hopeful through the long somber evenings.

"Mom! You can see your breath in the house!"

"Put on another sweater."

Now, under the darkness of the tall leafy maple tree behind our new home, surrounding the stones shining in the moonlight and the patio's pool of gray shadow, we have a white garden. White flowers hold light somehow. The blossoms shine in darkness, in hundreds of shades of pearl, ivory, mist, opal, and down feather, silvery white lace and warm thick cream. The bare dirt yard has become in such a short time a studied, sacred place. In the shade, woodland flowers live among the ferns. Behind the flowers, climbing hydrangeas, viburnum, and other white flowering vines and shrubs will create a background someday of deep and magical whites.

Like any good contemplative space, our garden has its apostolic ministry, especially to the neighborhood children. Max, age ten, loves working with Bill. During every outdoor project he chatters nonstop nearby. Max eagerly helps me with chores outdoors, but he also serves as a kind of spatial consultant. He will say, "Something's off here. This sidewalk in the backyard that came with the house—it doesn't go anywhere, does it? You need a focal point. How about a statue where the pavement ends, so it looks like the sidewalk's going somewhere?" Or, "See how nicely your lawn curves around in an oval shape—but then the eye gets confused. You need a small tree right here to complete the line...." Of course. So we let Max choose the place for the birch tree—a "focal point" seen through the rose bower that completes the curve of the oval lawn.

His sister Emma, age five, gets home from kindergarten at half past eleven, when Lady's deeply bred instincts compel her to herd the little girl off the bus and escort her safely home. But first Emma stops by our little pond to feed the goldfish, walk through the flowers, observe the pumpkin vine, smell the lemon thyme, and check for rose buds. Her sister Maddie, who is nine and less talkative, loves to keep me company. Maddie and I share a secret about the house. She weeds if I am weeding or digs if I am digging, and just smiles and smiles. I give Maddie, Max, and Emma my extra plants, and each of us is growing our own pumpkins, sunflowers, and pots of white pansies.

We love the fact that the neighborhood children share our garden with us. For Bill, the garden began as a necessary project because the house and yard were so appallingly neglected. I needed a garden to compensate for leaving the farmhouse with its magnificent view and solitude. But in less than a year, the yard has become one of the daily joys of being together as new husband and wife. We both delight in the beauty our work brings forth, and discover a common interest in the shared memory of planting bulbs or seeds or vines, and in giving the neighbors nearly as much delight as the garden gives us.

Such a small thing, sharing our garden! But this ongoing and living memory of planning, planting, watching, delighting, and sharing is a kind of *anamnesis*, which is a unique way to par-

43

ticipate in time. *Anamnesis* means to call to mind again, to remember. Gardening draws upon the kind of faith that remembers the past by offering beauty to the future while enjoying the moment.

44

This Greek word is used often in theology because it conveys so much more than the English word "memorial" or "remembrance." When Jesus says *Do this in remembrance of me* at his last supper, does he mean for us merely to remember his act of breaking bread and sharing cup with his disciples, or something more? The history of the church is stained with blood over the interpretation.

Because praying confronts us with the fragility of time at the edge of our own souls, I believe that time breaks down when we worship. Something extraordinary happens in the moment of remembrance: Jesus is here with us. Past and future are one as we taste the bread and wine, set apart by sacred time and place. I'm not sure I would even bother with church if I did not sense something vital and eternal in that moment.

Granted, I prepare all week so that during this particular, hushed point of the liturgy I will attend to it with all my spiritual, intellectual, and physical powers. In prayer this intense, past and future hardly exist. As a priest and teacher of children, my purpose in the church is to help prepare others for sacred moments.

Bill and Max, Emma, Maddie, and I each enjoy the garden at different times and in different ways, although we all delight in it one way or another, usually as we work in the moment. After all, it is the present, not the past or the future, that breaks into eternity.

When the climbing hydrangeas and viburnum mature, the shrubs will create a beautiful display of blossoms in summer, berries in fall, interesting shapes and seeds and pods in winter, and vigorous shoots of new green in spring. By that time, Bill and I will no longer live here. Someday, the birch trees will glow white in the night along with the white flowers. The lily of the valley, wood anemone, fern, and bloodroot will have spread throughout the shady berm. Happiness in this house will belong to another family. A new tenant may not like white flowers at all, and replace them, or mow down all the plants, or let them fall back into weeds. But I think that Max, Maddie, and Emma will remember their neighbors' unusual white garden.

No doubt some other family will have to build a shelter around the fig tree Uncle Andrew gave us when it grows too big for the basement. The thought delights me.

46

Almighty God our heavenly Father, you declare your glory and show forth your handiwork in the heavens and in the earth: Deliver us in our various occupations from the service of self alone, that we may do the work you give us to do in truth and beauty and for the common good; for the sake of him who came among us as one who serves, your Son Jesus Christ our Lord, who lives and reigns with you and the Holy Spirit, one God, for ever and ever. Amen.

collect for vocation in daily work,
BCP 261

five

Mapping

The Timepiece of the Hours

And God said, "Let there be lights in the dome of the sky to separate the day from the night; and let them be for signs and for seasons and for days and years, and let them be lights in the dome of the sky to give light upon the earth." And it was so.

Genesis 1:14-15

N ow that I am used to the space within and around my new home, and I can absent-mindedly find my coffee or car keys, I begin to think about praying in time. How do the predictable rhythms of my work day create a pattern of light and movement and sound in which I can build a life of prayer?

On a three-by-five card I regularly create a "map" for the day: a list of things I have to do, where I have to go to do them, and the names of the people I have to call on the telephone: *Shop Rite, Home Depot, bank, copy shop, church.* Then I create boxes of sublists within the day map, a bird's-eye view of details to take care of in different places—like the city streets that are inset on a state highway map. *Church: set Jacob and Esau costumes, work on Erin's notebook, give Steve music, meet with Frank 2 P.M.* I try all the while to allow for interruptions, emergencies, diversions. As long as I don't misplace my card, I don't have to clutter my brain with things I have to remember. Sometimes I remember to pray and sometimes I schedule times for prayer: *5 P.M. monastery vespers.* My map is a kind of clock, a timepiece of hours for places and tasks: time to go

48

to church, time to go home. And with prayer scheduled into my day, like waltzes on a dance card, I enter a different sphere of time.

When and wherever I pray, I sit and listen first. At home I hear the familiar sounds of the highway, the dog sighing in her sleep at my feet, children playing in the street, a muffled television set downstairs. At the monastery I listen to the ceiling fan in the chapel, footsteps in the hall by the bell rope, birds chattering in the ivy, the train whistle across the river. From my basement room at the church I listen to the voices of staff and visitors, phones ringing, occasional laughter. I recognize the different clicking toenail sounds on the parish hall floor: the priest's excitable little dog, the choirmaster's gentle reserved dog, the bishop's large elderly dog. I am grateful in the moment for the sounds distinctive to each place over which I have no immediate responsibility.

Then sometimes when I pray, I enter the sphere behind the sounds: an alternative sphere of time and presence. I want to tell the children I teach, "When you pray, you are a time traveler!"

Sun and moon, constellations and planets in their courses are all timepieces set in a universe that once gave birth to time. From this outermost spiral arm of the Milky Way, we tell time by watching the sky. The rotation of the earth defines day and night, the vast elliptical journey around the sun, the years. The tilting of the planet's axis initiates the seasons, while the gentle waxing and waning moon in its arc across the night sky guides planting and harvest, religious feasts and fasts.

The ziggurats of Babylon, the standing stones of prehistoric Celtic lands, Aztec observatories, the constellations—these measured time for our ancient ancestors. Today I take for granted the radio's BBC news Greenwich mean time "pips" on my radio, and my computer set precisely to the United States Naval Observatory clock. I draw my own map of time in the morning on my index cards after consulting my calendar. I am disoriented during the day without my wristwatch.

Other timepieces also guide my little world. My own body is a timepiece worn by gravity. My stubby and freckled hand, clasping this pen clumsily between swollen joints, discloses the number of my years. A petal fallen from the freesia blossom to the lace on my desk reminds me of life yielding to death. The blinking digits of my alarm clock, pulsating more precisely than my heartbeat as I write, inform me second by second of the length and transience of day and night.

My breathing, so many breaths per minute, measures the dimensions of movement and becoming—except when I forget to breathe and have to catch up. The yellowing wallpaper with its brown seams forces me to think of the future: I need to put *Call the wallpaper lady* on my next map list! A cache of sad letters Bill found behind the wallboards in the attic incites my curiosity about the past in this house. The pattern of cars to and fro on the street, the beep! beep! at ten of nine, the step of the mailman, the train whistle; the sticky trail of the garden snail and the impossible beat of wings of the hummingbird, the jasmine blooming in the bathroom in December and the hundreds of bulbs asleep under the snow: all are timepieces in my little universe.

Because of prayer, I cannot quite let go of the feeling that chronological time is an illusion even though time, as strong and sure as gravity, pulls away my life day by day. Sagging flesh and wrinkles and a crown of gray hair mock my sense in prayer that mortal life is not as real as the unseen sphere behind the boundary of the soul. Prayer ushers the soul through the threshold of the present moment into sacred time.

If time is the dimension of becoming, mystical union with God is the purpose of becoming. God is the eternal present, the beginning and ending, the Alpha and the Omega. That is why St. Paul could write:

> For I am convinced that neither death, nor life, nor angels, nor rulers, nor things present, nor things to come, nor powers, nor height, nor depth, nor anything else in all creation, will be able to separate us from the love of God in Christ Jesus our Lord. (Romans 8:38-39)

A friend recently died after seven years of an unrelenting battle with cancer, leaving behind a wife and three children. At the funeral his priest observed that our friend had finally become more interested in the Healer than in being healed. By gazing straight into death, he transcended death before he died. Mystical union dissolves the boundary between death and life; we become one with the Healer, rather than merely healed. By dying in divine love, we inherit eternal love.

Many people come to the love of God as human love fails. Others realize their dependence upon God as illness finally shatters the illusion of independence. And many acquire knowledge of the power of God when the loss of money shatters the illusion of power. So also, entering the present reality of time in prayer reveals the hidden gate into eternal time.

The ordinary day is a vehicle of transcendence, hour by hour; the Christian prayer hours, a timepiece of eternity. To subvert time, we must enter into time itself. For engaging the sense of reality behind time in prayer does not require that we learn to walk in two worlds at the same time, but rather that we learn to walk in two times in the same world.

O Lord God Almighty, as you have taught us to call the evening, the morning, and the noonday one day; and have made the sun to know its going down: Dispel the darkness of our hearts, that by your brightness

*we may know you to be the true God and
eternal light, living and reigning for ever
and ever. Amen.*

prayer for light,
BCP 110

II

Praying in Time

six

Sleeping
The Hour of Vigils

Early in the morning I cry out to you,
　for in your word is my trust.
My eyes are open in the night watches,
　that I may meditate upon your promise.
Psalm 119:147-148

T he purpose of a vigil is to await a certain
time or event. The purpose of the Christian
hour of Vigils is to await time itself.

The ancient monastic practice of rising some-
time between midnight and two in the morning to
pray sanctifies the night hours. To me the idea of
nuns and monks rising from their beds in the middle of the night and shuffling down a darkened
hall in pairs by candlelight, half asleep, to sing
and pray in a cold chapel is both appalling and
comforting.

The practice appalls me because I cannot
imagine myself rising voluntarily in the night.
Those times when I have been sleep deprived, I
have seen phantasms, heard horrible voices, and
once encountered the very devil himself breaking
into my bedroom, unkempt and dirty in old beard
stubble and camouflage battle fatigues. A week in
a noisy hospital ward summons the Four
Horsemen of the Apocalypse right to the foot of
my bed to argue over how to take the world.

Frankly, I think I would be stark raving mad if
my sleep were regularly interrupted for prayer in
the middle of the night. As a mother, I have no
memory at all of my second child's first year when

he could not sleep through the night while the oldest, an active toddler, stayed awake by day. My daughter Grace did not sleep soundly until she was four years old. And when she turned five I had another baby. Those times of habitual sleep deprivation exhausted my mind and emotions as well as my body. But I am assured by monks and nuns who keep Vigils in their community that the body and mind do adjust.

When I visit Suk-Hui, a friend of mine who is a flight attendant, she offers me jam from London, wine from Paris, chocolates from Belgium, coffee from Costa Rica, and other exotic delicacies she "picked up" in other time zones. Her days off are spent adjusting to time differences through a rigorous discipline of diet, including abstinence from caffeine and wine, and refraining from sleep no matter how tired she is until she can make up the right amount of hours at the right time. Thank goodness pilots and police, mothers and doctors, nuclear plant operators and monks and nuns, and all those who work while others sleep learn to adjust to the rigors of disrupted time.

Beyond these ascetic adjustments and my memories of sleep deprivation, however, the image of nuns and monks singing in the cold chapel in the middle of the night is comforting. I know a practiced spirit stands as a sentry on the boundary of the soul, watching the horizon for danger or delight. The nun intentionally watches for the end of time. The monk fixes his inward gaze toward the horizon to watch for the Second Coming of the Christ.

> For you yourselves know very well that the day of the Lord will come like a thief in the night.... So then let us not fall asleep as others do, but let us keep awake and be sober. (1 Thessalonians 5:2, 6)

And my monk and nun friends all assure me that if they see anything, they will call me right away.

Hippolytus, writing in the third century, admonished all Christians to rise about midnight, wash their hands with water, and pray before going back to bed again. Even children were encouraged to arise with their parents to develop the habit of watching for Christ in the night. I would never purposely wake a child who had the good sense to sleep through the night, but singing hymns to a child disturbed by bad dreams or a stomach ache counts, I think.

Waking in the night for prayer does, however, prepare you for other disruptions in time and routine. If you are used to turning your attention toward Christ whenever you rise, then when the call comes to be at the bedside of a dying friend or to rescue a stranded daughter when her car breaks down, the prayer you have developed precedes your response. Spontaneously, from the habit of nocturnal prayer, you will commend to Christ your waking hours and the friend or child or relative or victim. And when the crisis of the darkest hour is at hand, and you are asked to *remain here and watch with me* (Matthew 26:38), the obedience bred of years of practice will allow you to rise to face that hour.

A friend of mine who is a hermit calls Vigils "the prayer office for pious insomniacs." On a more serious note, though, many religious people are wakened by the Spirit in the middle of the night in order to pray for someone in need. It is a common experience among Christians to discover that at the exact hour when someone needing to be commended to God was ministered to, a friend was raised from sleep on the other side of the globe. A nun once told me about the uncanny intuitiveness of people in parts of Africa, where she served for many years. "People knew of things even before the drumming began," she said. "This knowing is not such a miracle. It is simply that here in the west, we have forgotten how to be connected."

The formal service of Vigils was inspired not only by the imminence of the Second Coming, and thus the need to be prepared either for disruption or for the possibilities of grace, but also by the text of Psalm 119: *At midnight I will rise to give you thanks, because of your righteous judgments* (v. 62). The hour of Vigils is the eighth hour, the night office, which is balanced against the seven traditional offices that make up the day's hours.

A Jewish midrash tradition on this psalm text has King David suspending a harp over his bed before he sleeps. When the north wind stirs at midnight, the melody of the wind playing through the strings of the instrument awakens David. He rises to study the Torah. When his subjects learn that their king rises at midnight to study they declare, "If David, King of Israel, is studying the Torah, how much more should we!" And they too immediately rise from their beds to study in the night.

To rise in the night to give thanks is a sacrifice indeed. Even if God dwells beyond time, God must know that we dwell in time, and for us to rise in the night under any circumstance, painful or joyful, is an extraordinary exercise. Although I learned to stash my spiritual reading near the rocking chair during the years of getting up in the night with four babies, now I prefer my cocoon of heavy quilts and comforters all through the night. Like the question asked during the Passover meal, "Why do we recline instead of being ready, staff in hand and foot raised, ready to escape from the oppressors in Egypt?" The answer? Because we can! We recline to emphasize the luxury of our peace and stability. Even though I sleep all night now that my children are grown, because I can, I still remember that even asleep the soul must be turned to God. So I commend myself to God in prayer before I sleep.

Something of our soul will remain linked to that warm darkness beyond its boundary, even in sleep. This dark love, more intimate than a mother's womb, nourishes, encourages, and guides us, enveloping us in its loving, wordless darkness. When we pay attention, and respond with wordless, loving prayer in the darkness of our souls, we know we are connected to divine life. When we commend our souls to God at night, we take this connection for granted. Awake or asleep, we live in the Lord.

> *Guide us waking, O Lord, and guard us sleeping; that awake we may watch with Christ, and asleep we may rest in peace.*

> antiphon at the conclusion of Compline,
> BCP 134

seven

Waking

The Hour of Matins

Sleeper, awake!
  Rise from the dead,
and Christ will shine on you.

Ephesians 5:14

My husband rarely remembers his dreams. He wakes instantly and bolts out of bed and into his clothes, ready for the day's adventures. Unlike Bill, I can hardly distinguish dream from reality. My spirit wanders in foreign galaxies, embodying unfamiliar forms, while in my dreams I speak in tongues of neither men nor angels: I am a voice whimpering in the wilderness between sleep and waking.

It seems to me that I travel extensive distances to find my way home to this outer arm of lonely stars in the Milky Way. That I consistently find myself back in the same body every day, of all the bodies on earth, surprises me—although sometimes I return to my bed from nothing less mundane than missed high school classes or college credits, or taking exams unprepared. At other times my dreams are horrifying and disturbing. Still, waking always surprises me.

I emerge from the dark universe and through the desert wilderness to the hum of an electric toothbrush: my son is getting ready for school. I hear the click of the front door and creak of the porch steps as Bill and Lady go outside for a walk. Bill always knows who he is and where he is going, but I must come in from the outer reaches of the universe and cross a desert threshold in the time he takes to go downstairs and put on his jacket.

Like some desperate lost soul emerging from a tunnel of Hades, suddenly reprieved from death, I come to consciousness, eyes blinking from the surprise of morning light. I remember. I wake to worship. *Open my lips, O Lord, and my mouth shall proclaim your praise,* I finally say. Or whisper. Or whimper. Or just think to myself and to the Blessed Holy One who hears whether I say the words aloud or, like the Spirit itself, groan inwardly with sighs too deep for words.

In the morning, LORD, you hear my voice; early in the morning I make my appeal and watch for you (Psalm 5:3). The original Hebrew, however, is more ambiguous than the prayer book translation. Another translation reads, *At daybreak you listen for my voice,* as if the psalmist is saying that God waits and listens for that first word of prayer before anything else can happen. Does God wait to hear my timid whisper?

If so, the balance between my life and death hangs in that silence before coming to consciousness. The blinking eyes, the sigh, the yawn. The taking in of breath to speak. God straining, perhaps, to find a hint of will within my weakness, to listen for my voice.

In monastic culture, Matins consecrates the day to God. But even before a monk or nun joins in the communal office of Matins at dawn in the chapel, his or her first impulse of thought and quickening of heart should be consecrated to God. As early monastic writer John Cassian said in his conferences on prayer, the stretching forth of hands, the bending of the knee, the rising from bed to stand, the first motion of the tongue, "the door of lips singing hymns"—all should be offered as "a sacrifice of joy."

Waking from sleep is waking from death: consciousness, the paradigm of resurrection. Aside from the basic instincts of human survival and procreation, perhaps the only meaning in life is this metaphor of learning to wake to consciousness of God. Setting apart the day prepares the soul for deification, transformation, resurrection. Maybe waking is just practice. Someday I will die and I will know how to wake to resurrection consciousness. Perhaps I will wake fully into the sphere of God because I have practiced Matins. I am often afraid, walking in those dark worlds of bad dreams, but God may give me bad dreams for an urgent reason: to learn to wake as I might in worlds to come, wholly and completely.

The neighborhood wakes. First to small bathroom lights, then kitchen lights. The highway roars with commerce, commuters, an occasional siren. A dog barks. An old station wagon across the street groans unwillingly to the turn of the key. Like silent shades, high school students float through mist toward the bus stop in front of the church at the bottom of our street. A whistle foretells the arrival of the train into Poughkeepsie: long, long, short, long. The scrape of snow shovel on a sidewalk. The thwack of a newspaper hitting a porch door. Two short whistles announce the Metro North leaving the station for New York City.

Dawn will come soon over the rise at the top of the street. Inside I hear the sink, the shower, the refrigerator door. I smell coffee, oatmeal, eggs. My son's backpack drops to the floor as he puts on his boots. I listen for the steps of my husband returning to our porch and the click of Lady's paws eagerly coming through the front door to find me. Lady knows who she is, sleeping and waking, and she would not care where in the universe she lived as long as she had people or cows to herd. I am her lone cow, whom she must diligently herd into the study so that I may continue to awake into prayer.

70

> *Lord God, almighty and everlasting Father, you have brought us in safety to this new day: Preserve us with your mighty power, that we may not fall into sin, nor be overcome by adversity; and in all we do, direct us to the fulfilling of your purpose; through Jesus Christ our Lord. Amen.*
>
> a collect for grace,
> BCP 100

eight

Reading

The Hour of Lauds

Early on the first day of the week, while it was still dark, Mary Magdalene came to the tomb. . . .

John 20:1

While it is still dark, Lady noses me into my study. I start my little coffee-maker, which sounds like a child slurping the remains of a bubbly ice cream float through a straw. In my study the uneasy remnants of my dreams dwindle and dissolve, and specters slide from me. The transparent images fade into the light. My mind is eager. My mind is hungrier than my body.

I am a cheerful riser. I think most clearly after the dreams have fallen away and before I remember everything I have to do this day and week. I am so grateful that I can read at this time because when my children were little I could not read in the mornings. If I so much as stirred from the bed, crises in multiples of four erupted upon me. For twenty-five years dawn has meant a crisis of homework, shoes, or permission slips; raging hunger, accidental breakage, or occasional vomiting—often mine. This is the first time in over two decades I do not have to drive children to school or the bus stop.

Patrick, the one child left at home, noisily brushes his teeth and braces, cooks his own breakfast, organizes his homework, and rarely forgets anything. All I have to do in the morning is check the neatness of his hair and make sure he does not wear his old ripped sweatshirt to school. Bill, having already jumped into his clothes, prefers to take care of himself and does not need to be fussed over. All I see of him this morning is a smile as he kisses me goodbye and rushes off.

And so, God gets this time—my best time of day! The hour of Lauds is praise for this very hour before dawn, and the theme is thanksgiving, gratitude for surviving the night, another chance to learn and to love. Lauds is praise for the coming dawn, which represents the creation of the world and the resurrection of Jesus. Christ is the morning star, and the sun is the glory of the Lord God. *Arise, shine; for your light has come, and the glory of the LORD has risen upon you* (Isaiah 60:1).

To study and pray at the moment of creation, at the garden tomb of Jesus, creates a sense of sheer grace for me. While frenzied birds sing the dawn into being, I mold my body into my son Jack's "favorite chair in all the world": a slightly undersized, fuzzy brown rocker covered with a beige blanket and an old lace tablecloth. It is a mom-reading-to-kids or cuddling-kids-and-puppies kind of chair, big enough to curl up with my feet under me and small enough for my feet to touch the floor. And my gratitude is clearly enhanced by coffee.

The combination of the scent of coffee, the lamp switched on over the chair, and the unzipping of the Bible case signals Lady that it is the time for her daily bone. She jumps and dances until I give her the fresh rawhide twisted into knots on two ends. (She won't chew on straight rawhide sticks or boring rectangles.) She takes it to her rug and then works and worries over that bone with paws and jaws until it is soft, deconstructed. Lady reads, marks, learns, swallows, and inwardly digests. The fragments left over go into a basket of bone remnants. These she shuns like yesterday's newspapers—though occasionally a small piece will seem to evoke some interest, like a savory passage in a discarded diary.

Dogs don't worship as humans do, and dogs probably don't pray. Nevertheless her example helps me work a bit more doggedly than I might otherwise. So I work and worry lovingly over a passage in the Bible in order to learn the story, to discern the allegory, to sense the heavenly directives and listen to the Dark Love in secret behind the text.

Whenever I look up from my reading, I see a crown of thorns, a jar, a hollow-blown egg dyed red and resting on a bit of lace on the shelf—all symbols representing Mary Magdalene. They make a "beautiful corner," fashioned after the ones in Russian homes, and not unlike a Latino or Hindu home altar. I still look for the proper icon for my beautiful corner.

I named my house Magdala. The village of Magdala nestles at the bottom of a unique mountain plateau on the Sea of Galilee. I saw it for the first time from a boat on the Sea of Galilee, but the village can be seen from Capernaum and from the Mount of Beatitudes. So my room honors Mary of Magdala, the hermit and apostle.

This is the secret I share with my neighbor Maddie. Her given name is Madeline. When we first moved here, the neighborhood children were busy looking up the meaning of their names and Maddie was disappointed. "It means a girl from a town called Magdala. What's that supposed to mean?" she sulked.

Ah, Madeline! Wait until I unpack and show you the books and pictures I have of a wonderful woman from Magdala! She was the first to see Jesus after his resurrection from the dead. She was the apostle to the apostles. She was Jesus' special friend. She became a great teacher. According to some legends, she lived the rigorous and brave life of a hermit in the desert; according to others, she preached all over the known world about the risen Christ. The next few days I notice that Maddie walks slowly to and from school, smiling and pointing at my house while holding her mother's hand.

I love all the stories about this Mary, sinner and saint, including the medieval romantic fantasies that describe the wedding at Cana as the nuptial feast of Mary of Magdala and John the beloved disciple. After Jesus changes to water to wine, John leaves the feast and his new bride to follow Jesus. The furious young Mary turns to a life of prostitution until she, too, becomes a disciple and dies in Patmos as part of the community gathered around John the gospel writer and evangelist. So my little house in the village becomes Magdala, a place to go out into the world from, preaching and teaching. But I love Mary especially for the moment at dawn before she hears her own name spoken by the one she loves.

When Jesus' body had been taken down from the cross, his friends hurriedly washed and tended the corpse until the last moment before the Sabbath, when righteous Jews must refrain from such work. His body lay in the tomb throughout the evening, the day of Sabbath, and the night following. But at the first possible moment after the holy time set apart for observance, on the first day of the week, before dawn, Mary Magdalene returns to the tomb to finish anointing the body of her beloved friend. She comes to the grave, expecting nothing, simply to complete the burial ritual. It is dark and she is there.

This moment in scripture, above all metaphors and stories, reveals my inmost life of prayer. It is dark. I am here. It is enough. I expect nothing, not even my name whispered in the dark. I simply know I must be here, in faith, before dawn.

The sun rises, morning comes, and I break my reverie. I must eat and dress. Eating and dressing complete the hour of Lauds for me.

My Buddhist friends tell me to chew my food mindfully, savoring every moment and motion of my mouth and jaw and throat. But most often I eat while listening to world news on the radio and brushing my hair and dressing. My fiber-rich cereal takes a lot of chewing, mindful or not, and too often I take for granted the goodness of the grains from the midwest, raisins from California, coconut from Hawaii, soy milk from Michigan, sunflower nuts from Kansas, and bananas from Latin America. Bill composes this cereal for me from a dozen sources and mixes the ingredients in a plastic jug. The cereal reminds me of the noise on the highway—all those trucks screeching back and forth bringing products from here to there. Here is where apples come from. There is where my soy milk comes from. And the delicious coconut. Not to mention the miracle of coffee.

After living with the capricious plumbing of my old farmhouse, the hot shower here is still a novelty. Humidity and a sunny south window make this cramped little bathroom the perfect place for a jasmine vine, even though the room is already small and crowded with toilet, sink, and tub. I love it this tiny bathroom. Someone sent me this prayer from the Talmud:

> When we go to the bathroom, we say to the two angels who are always with us: Guard me, guard me. Help me, help me. Be reliable, be reliable. Wait for me, wait for me, until I go in and come out—for this is what human beings must do. (Berachot 60)

I don't mind the angels coming in with me, even if it is crowded. The angels can admire the jasmine while I shower.

Showered, dressed, and ready to go to work, I will soon become part of the noisy traffic on Route 9W. Now is the time I try to remember to consecrate my day to God, because for sure I will forget to live in the presence of God once I am on the road.

O God, the King eternal, whose light divides the day from the night and turns the shadow of death into the morning: Drive far from us all wrong desires, incline our hearts to keep your law, and guide our

*feet into the way of peace; that, having
done your will with cheerfulness during the
day, we may, when night comes, rejoice to
give you thanks; through Jesus Christ our
Lord. Amen.*

80

a collect for the renewal of life,
BCP 99

nine

Worship
The Hour of Terce

In the last days it will be, God declares, that I will pour out my Spirit upon all flesh, and your sons and your daughters shall prophesy, and your young men shall see visions, and your old men shall dream dreams. Even upon my slaves, both men and women, in those days I will pour out my Spirit; and they shall prophesy. And I

will show portents in the heaven above
and signs on the earth below, blood, and
fire, and smoky mist. The sun shall be
turned to darkness and the moon to blood,
before the coming of the Lord's great and
glorious day. Then everyone who calls on
the name of the Lord shall be saved.

Acts 2:17-21

B ecause I live right next to a highway I can be
almost anywhere I might need to go quickly,
like Mary Magdalene in her skiff on the
Mediterranean. I can be at the train station in
Poughkeepsie in ten minutes, New Paltz in fifteen
minutes, or Kingston, where I work, in twenty-
five minutes. I also live near Holy Cross
Monastery, a Benedictine Episcopal religious
community for men, so even if I am still brushing
my teeth or hair during the eight o'clock news, I
can be in the monastery chapel by a quarter past
eight for the daily eucharist.

Worship

For ten years I have prayed in this chapel. My prayer rises and shapes itself to the curves of the ceiling and arches. Here my prayer is as simple as the white walls and the Romanesque design. The stone floor where I sit when I am alone is as familiar as any place I have ever lived. I know the ceiling fan tone, which is a perfect fifth, the sputter and bangs and hiss of the steam radiators in winter, and the chattering of sparrows in the ivy when summer comes. I am used to the train whistle across the river, creaks in the floor at someone's step, the sigh of a dog creeping in to lie down, an occasional soft snore, the deep bell calling guests and monks to prayer. I breathe the familiar scents of wood polish, wax, candles, sometimes flowers, and always the lingering scent of incense.

When I worked here I prayed daily as the bells rang for the offices, and monastic time began to influence the pace of my own soul's clock. For two years I answered the phone, sorted mail, prepared bills and letters, and took reservations for the guest house. I served as priest at the altar when it was my turn on the daily rota. My two younger children and I worshiped here on Sundays.

When you pray in one place for a long time, the prayers become one prayer. You come and go and life begets its drastic changes, but the same holy space receives your prayer. It is like someone being home at the kitchen table, waiting with the light on as you stumble and bump around doing your chores in the dark outside. And so I pray here whenever I can, alone or with others at the eucharist or the daily office. It is easy to pray in this place, not least of all because I can worship in community without having to be sociable. The monks have chapter, which is their community meeting, right after church and I can slip out the heavy back door without encountering guests.

Somehow the ritual of the eucharist focuses me in the morning. My heart dances the story of death to life, slavery to freedom, sin to redemption. I have danced Incarnation to Resurrection to Pentecost in forty-five minutes. The service is over by nine o'clock, the third hour of monastic prayer known as Terce. It is "the golden hour"—the hour of the Holy Spirit. Fifty days after the passover of Jesus' death, on the day of Pentecost, at nine in the morning, the disciples and friends and relatives of Jesus were in the upper room praying. The Holy Spirit came upon them suddenly, like the rush of a mighty wind filling the house. They were so giddy with ecstasy that everyone in the street outside thought they were drunk. The disciples found themselves speaking in many languages and understanding each one—a sign that they would go out to the ends of the earth, preaching with tongues of fire.

This is the moment the church bids us remember the disciples on fire with the Holy Spirit when we go off to work: *You will be my witnesses in Jerusalem, in all Judea and Samaria, and to the ends of the earth* (Acts 1:8). For me, the ends are Poughkeepsie, New Paltz, and Kingston. No place very exotic.

For those of us formed less by signs, wonders, and golden tongues than by mundane, working-class American life, I like the Shaker practice of asking for the gift your work will give you. "Put your hands to work and your heart to God," they say. Ask for a gift for this day, this week, this month, this year. Do you need patience? Ask the Holy Spirit to give you patience in your work. What about the seven gifts of the Holy Spirit—

wisdom, understanding, counsel, knowledge, ghostly strength, true godliness, or holy fear?

What lofty gifts! Lofty gifts of longtime goals. While the author of *The Cloud of Unknowing* can say, "short prayer pierces heaven," the monks counsel, "*Lento, lento,* slow and sure." The turtle soul plodding along finishes the course more surely than the erratic hare soul. The steadfastness of monastic time—the daily hours in steady doses rather than pastiches and sound bites for Sunday amusement or comfort—works deeply into the soul for gradual conversion and change. Let the faithful pilot light on the back burner purify our souls steadily, with occasional rises of heat and light but always gently, with constancy.

Give me those gifts that you would have in me, Lord. Let my life for you be like Jacob working seven years for his beloved Rachel: *they seemed to him but a few days because of the love he had for her* (Genesis 29:20). I invoke the Holy Spirit at this hour of the Holy Spirit. What gift should I ask for in my work today? What do I most need to serve you? What causes me the most pain when I think about it? What situation today do I most fear?

Worship

What I least look forward to today is a confrontation with the "continually complaining person." Every church has a continually complaining person or two: the fractious duo of ladies belittling the sermon in the parking lot after church; the sanctimonious vestryman on a lone crusade circulating a petition to drive you from your cure; the jealous, rumor-mongering diva hinting at scandalous fictions; the perpetual nay-sayer.

Now, good criticism saves time. A good critique or warning or suggestion at the beginning of a project can save untold hours of labor, make a weak program strong, cut through busywork, or save volunteers from overlapping tasks. But the habit of negativity can infiltrate any good thing and tear it asunder. You wait for that cymbal to drop in the orchestra pit during the tender love scene, and even if it does not drop just at that moment, you have been drawn into the habit of anticipating the crash. That idle comment behind your back, that undoing and unraveling, that habitual doubt-sowing by someone you hoped and expected would share the same desire: negative thinking sinks into walls and infects whole organizations, an unseen tumor strangling vital organs.

What will I bring to the rising of my prayer like incense at Vespers, my evening sacrifice, that will have yielded love and patience or the needed *bon mot?* Let me bring confrontation, if necessary. Let me bring the head of the dragon of naysaying to the evening sacrifice! Whatever it is, give me that gift for the sake of our little church program, for your sake, for your love's sake.

I know that in addition to remembering the Holy Spirit, the church offers a mixed message of ecstasy and dread at the hour of going to work. Terce traditionally recalls the hour of the condemned man, Jesus on the cross. Behold the man. The crown of thorns. The blindfolding and beating, the hitting, the spitting; the whipping until his flesh hung off his bones, sadistic yet merciful because the more severe the flaying, the sooner the death on the cross. Here is your king.

The passion of Jesus puts into perspective that one miniscule complaining church person. Terce reminds me why I am working at all. The mass has prepared me for my day by reminding me of the passion, the resurrection, and the windy, fiery

Worship

Holy Spirit's indwelling love. The eucharist has told me the whole story. Lord, give me that gift you would have me learn today. Give me that love you would have me give today. Slipping out the heavy back door of the monastery church, I get into my car and go to work.

89

> *Almighty and most merciful God, grant that by the indwelling of your Holy Spirit we may be enlightened and strengthened for your service; through Jesus Christ our Lord, who lives and reigns with you, in the unity of the Holy Spirit, one God, now and for ever. Amen.*

collect of the Holy Spirit,
BCP 251

ten

Working

The Hour of Sext

While I was on my way and approaching Damascus, about noon a great light from heaven suddenly shone about me. I fell to the ground and heard a voice saying to me, "Saul, Saul, why are you persecuting me?" I answered, "Who are you, Lord?" Then he said to me, "I am Jesus of Nazareth whom you are persecuting." Now those who were

with me saw the light but did not hear the
voice of the one who was speaking to me. I
asked, "What am I to do, Lord?" The Lord
said to me, "Get up and go to Damascus;
there you will be told everything that has
been assigned to you to do." Since I could
not see because of the brightness of that
light, those who were with me took my
hand and led me to Damascus.

Acts 22:6-11

The angelus bell at Holy Cross Church where
I work rings at noon. It is on a timer: three,
three, and three rings, then nine. At this moment
I am usually listening to public radio news. Right
after the angelus bell the Narcotics Anonymous
meeting begins. From my basement room I cannot
hear the words exactly, but only a muffled voice
reading a statement, the shifting of chairs, clap-
ping from time to time, footsteps to and from
the coffee machine, and, after an hour, a raucous
end to the meeting. At noon on Saturdays and

Working

Sundays the church hall is filled with neighbors who sit down for a hot meal provided by the parish.

The angelus bell reminds me to pray. Otherwise I would forget. Even with the noon meeting starting, even with the public radio news, even with the people lined up in the hall and outside waiting to sit down to eat, I forget to pray. And when I eat at church on Sunday I usually miss grace, because at noon I am still fussing around in the sacristy trying to get out of the church before the Baptists start worshiping. Bill, meanwhile, is cooking in the parish hall. He peels fifty pounds of potatoes on Fridays for the weekend meals. And though I am so very grateful for the life that I live, the life God has given me and Bill protects for me, I would forget to pray but for the angelus bell, which sounds so serious and deep and full of prayer.

At noon the church remembers Paul's conversion on the road to Damascus, when the sudden light of the resurrected Christ blinded his soul and transformed him forever. Just to make sure he would get the point, Christ blinded Paul for three days. And just to drive it home, the blinded Paul had to depend upon the hospitality of the Christians he was about to arrest. So Paul never forgot the light, nor did he let anyone else forget it.

Noon seems to be one of the busiest times of day at the church, and that is the point of this meditation. Sext is the working hour, the hour with no shadow, the hour of turning from morning to afternoon and rushing into nighttime. Compared to my orderly morning, I observe with wonder the afternoons and evenings at the church, the long workday too full of activity and meetings, crazy people and complaining people and needy people, mixed-up times and missed appointments and too many appointments or people just dropping in with no appointment, and too many groups meeting in too little space.

My colleague Frank is energized by this hubbub. I admire his ability to thrive on chaos. I am glad I am not the rector, with all this responsibility. I am the children's priest. I teach Bible to the children and help with their spiritual formation and prayer. I thrive on their wonder and the questions they ask. But I love watching all the activities of the church swirling around me and not being in charge.

An artist-in-residence program is held here, so every couple of weeks the church is turned into a theater with props, costumes, banks of lights, platforms, scenery. The church hosts extremely talented composers, artists, singers, and actors. Suddenly an orchestra materializes: chairs, stands, tympani, violin cases, cellos, bass cases, and musicians in tuxedos. Or choruses, choirs, readings. A large swing band rehearses in the sanctuary on Monday nights. Then there is the smorgasborg of other activities: a bowling league, Al-Anon, the Baptist Bible School.

Other ministries with a wider scope are also housed at Holy Cross. The bishop coadjutor of New York has an office here, and so does Val, the Mid-Hudson Region's administrator, who sings in the choir and cooks food for the weekend dinners and holds one-third of the Diocese of New York together with compassion, wisdom, humor, discretion, and fervor. For the first time in a parish setting, I am aware of what is happening in the rest of the diocese and church. Clergy drop in. You can bump into a bishop. You can read the pastoral frustration, sadness, and joy on Val's face. I pray now for the larger church community because I am not isolated; I find I care more about the life and work of the diocese. Val loves the angelus bell for the same reason I do. "It brings me back to reality. We aren't here to push paper, we're here for the church and the church is here for us. The bell makes me remember in the middle of the day what all this fuss is about."

Several women run an active thrift shop that makes money for the church, and they generously gave me a room behind the shop for a children's program. We painted and carpeted and repaired. You have to walk through the thrift shop and, during the week, through a rack of winter coats, like the closet leading into Narnia, to get to my room.

I "prayed the place up" before I moved in, and noticed a peculiar impression in my prayer. Finally, I talked to the rector about it. "This is going to sound weird, Frank, but I keep thinking of St. Anne when I pray in that room." St. Anne is the apocryphal grandmother of Jesus and mother of Mary. Her shrines are places of healing. Her symbols are a lily and a book—and I suspect that if some artists had not been paid to be pious they might have more realistically portrayed Anne chasing the adolescent Mary around with that book in her hand! DaVinci portrays Grandma Anne just having a good time with the baby Jesus and a happy mother Mary. That was after all the unpleasantness over illegitimacy, however. Holy Cross's stained glass window shows a vacant-eyed, teenaged Mary on the cusp of sexiness and an anxious, tight-lipped mother Anne.

"That doesn't surprise me," Frank replied. "Do you know about the nuns? The Order of St. Anne? They used to teach the children in this church. They had an orphanage nearby. The nuns' ministry to children is still very much present in the older generation here."

"Oh." Of course—the prayers of those nuns are still lingering in the basement.

Now my room is full of costumes, props, books, maps, my collection of foreign dolls, and a display of nature artifacts: shells, rocks, bird nests, feathers, snake skins, animal skulls, bones, and fossils. The ceiling is strung with tiny white Christmas lights to represent God's covenant with Abraham: *Look toward heaven and count the stars, if you are able to count them.... So shall your descendants be* (Genesis 15:5). A mosquito net serves as the tent of the patriarchs, the Holy of Holies, a wedding canopy, the pillar of cloud, the cloud resting on Mt. Sinai, or the cloud of the Transfiguration—depending on what's going on. It is also a favorite place for kids to sit on a pile of pillows.

My room can be the meeting place at Shechem or the catacombs in Rome. And now we have an icon of St. Anne. The work we do in this room shapes the imagery of our prayer and, I hope, continually widens the vistas of our souls. Our play is work and our work is play. In my work, Sext is the hour of preparation for this playtime.

A typical Bible study with children works this way. We read aloud a story, usually from a children's book—secular or religious, it doesn't matter. The words, rhythm, sense of story, and our imagination all help us prepare for scripture study. Next we might discuss how our week's prayer life, Lenten discipline, or Advent family ceremony is going. Then we read a text from the Bible. To me the actual words and phrases are important and I never skip them, although I might explain as I go along. The children ask questions, and we decide how many parts or characters we need for our "play." If there are not enough characters to pretend in a story, a person may be an object, such as the golden calf or the stormy sea or a rainbow.

This afternoon we read together the story of the man born blind. In this story from the ninth chapter of the gospel of John, Jesus heals a blind man. First he spits on the ground, makes a paste with the saliva and dirt, and spreads the mud on the man's eyes. Then Jesus tells him to wash his eyes in the pool of Siloam. When the man returns, he is able to see. Later, the Pharisees call him into the synagogue for a hostile interview.

"Do you mean to tell me this man hocked up a loogey, put it on your eyes, and now you can see?" demands Emma, a tiny, ballet-dancing fourth grader with thick glasses and braces, transformed into a formidable Pharisee. The mother of the Man Born Blind in our play, *a.k.a.* mother of Emma, is overcome with embarrassment over her daughter's choice of words during Bible study. She shrinks even lower as the Pharisees press her for information about the healing. "Ask *him*, he's of age!" she whimpers to the Pharisees.

Billy plays the Man Born Blind as an irascible grouch. He reminds me of some of the men at the VA hospital in California where I did my clinical pastoral training. In the evening I would visit those being operated on the next day, wearing my little cross around my neck, and as soon as they perceived I was from the chaplain service—oh, the yelling and abuse! Like them, Billy the Man Born Blind abuses everybody: the Pharisees, his parents, and even Jesus, whose sacred spit brought light to his soul. Billy's blind man worships Jesus for about fifteen seconds and then acts as if he has never seen a miracle before. It is one of the best sermons I have ever seen.

Bible study is like the angelus bell—and I am like Billy's Man Born Blind. Unlike St. Paul, I tend to live as if I have never seen a miracle. The children teach me. I need the angelus bell to open my inner eye and wake me again to the presence of God.

Working

> *O God of peace, who hast taught us that in returning and rest we shall be saved, in quietness and in confidence shall be our strength: By the might of thy Spirit lift us, we pray thee, to thy presence, where we may be still and know that thou art God; through Jesus Christ our Lord. Amen.*

100

prayer for quiet confidence,
BCP 832

eleven

Coping
The Hour of None

One day Peter and John were going up to the temple at the hour of prayer, at three o'clock in the afternoon. And a man lame from birth was being carried in. People would lay him daily at the gate of the temple called the Beautiful Gate so that he could ask for alms from those entering the temple. When he saw Peter and John about to go into the temple, he asked them for alms. Peter looked intently at him, as did John, and said, "Look at us." And he fixed his attention on them, expecting to receive something from them. But Peter said, "I have no silver or gold, but what I have I give you; in the name of Jesus Christ of Nazareth, stand up and walk." And he took him by the right hand and raised him up; and immediately his feet and ankles were made strong. Jumping up, he stood and began to walk, and he entered the temple with them, walking and leaping and praising God.

Acts 3:1-8

W hat is the hardest thing about monastic life?" I love asking this question. I ask monks and nuns, novices, an elderly professed who took vows before I was born. Sometimes the answer comes quickly, with a glint in the eye like that of a would-be comedian hanging around the subway at Columbus Circle, hoping someone will ask, "How do you get to Carnegie Hall?" Then the long-awaited moment to deliver the old punch line, "Practice, my child, practice."

"What is the hardest thing about monastic life?"

"Other people," is the usual reply.

Church would be fine without other people. Unfortunately, the church simply *is* other people— a kind of purgatory, a rock garden of seedling souls in need of maturation. And because Jesus came not to call the righteous but sinners, the church is an interdependent root system of sinners who are all taking up the same water and soil from, in theologian Paul Tillich's words, "the infinite ground of all being."

By mid-afternoon, the whole process of being church with other people gets very tiresome. Tensions build. You want to just slap that continually complaining person. The impulse to rush through the rest of the day's work so that you can go home early threatens to deprive the garden of the living water meant to nourish at this very time of day. The hour of None is precisely the moment to stop and pray, think, and have a cup of tea.

So you pray. "Hey, wait a minute! Church is supposed to be a reflection of paradise, the heavenly Jerusalem here on earth. Where did all these weeds come from? When did the devil wake up from his hangover and plant these thistles around the fig tree? What's happening here?"

St. Paul complains to Barnabas that he won't travel ever, ever again with John Mark. Paul and Peter are wearing out the old argument about eating with gentiles. Meanwhile, Peter is preaching the case for circumcision and costing the church numerous pledgers, who are going back to the old shrines to give their money to Mithras. Peter complains that John's church is far too liberal. John's own parishioners acknowledge that he may be a great poet, but he is a terrible administrator.

"I'd rather have our dreamy John than your autocratic Peter."

"Yeah? At least we know how Peter stands on issues!"

"I'm sure you agree that the Magdalene woman is a loose cannon."

"She proves the point the church should require preachers to be licensed!"

Coping

"You know, I've had it with all the widows and orphans coming to church just for free food. I'm not going to host the teaching and fellowship, the breaking of bread and the prayers at my house any more."

"I see your point. And don't you agree that the kiss of peace is getting a bit too friendly?"

Sometimes people stalk away and leave the church. And sometimes that is very good for the church. These small, hot-house rebellions against the priest, or to gain control of the altar guild budget, erupt and dissolve with the waxing and waning moon. Maybe you have the temperament to worship with John's people. Maybe you are called to serve in Peter's church. Some stay, some leave. The tabs on my seed flats say, "Pulling apart the seedlings stimulates root growth." On the other hand, if you are a continually complaining person and you keep leaving churches because of the other people, then you are missing the point.

Within Benedictine monastic orders, the vow of stability anticipates the urge to flee. The brother you endured through postulancy and novitiate and the taking of vows shares your choir stall forever. His propensity not to wash after garden work, his morning halitosis, the perpetually irritating clearing of his throat during the Great Silence, his way of singing just enough off pitch to bring the choir down a fraction of a tone at each psalm phrase—all of this and more you have promised to endure for the rest of time through your vow of stability! And maybe even for the heavenly choir of eternity, too, unless God heals problems with body odor and musical pitch at the time of death.

On the other hand, monks are trained to look into the heart and soul of an annoying brother to find the treasured pearl of great price—perhaps a heroic generosity, or the ability to forgive, laugh, love, or bake a mean pecan pie. God wants this man here for some holy purpose. A treasure hidden in a field of annoying habits.

Watching monks chant in unison without driving each other to madness or murder is a revelation, a spiritual lesson not sold in bookstores. Monastic literature abounds with advice on transforming each irritation into an opportunity for sanctity and blessing. And no wonder. The vow of stability—staying in one monastic house or

106

order—teaches you to calculate the cost of
redemption in the most mundane of circumstances. If the church is other people, you simply
have to learn to cope.

Peter and John are going up to the temple at
the hour of prayer. None, the ninth hour, the
grouchy and irritable hour. Peter says, "Oh, no,
there's that continually complaining person waiting for us at the gate."

"Are we going to give him money?" asks John.

"No. Let's try something different today," says
Peter. The beggar fixes his attention upon Peter
and John, expecting to receive something from
them.

What is it that the continually complaining
person wants, anyway? Attention? To be important? Connection of some kind? Power? Healing?
Transformation?

"I don't have silver or gold, but I give you
what I have," offers Peter.

What do I have that I can give? Patience? A listening heart? A smile or laugh? Confrontation?
Endurance? Can I endure this person long enough
for him to cultivate the garden of his soul, to tend
to the "weeding out of vices and the planting of

virtues," as the monks put it? Can I endure long enough for her to be healed of that nagging, angry longing for the Lord? Can he endure me long enough for God to heal whatever it is in me that really bugs him?

I'll make a cup of tea, go out to the parish garden, and pull a weed or two while I think about it. The parish garden or monastery cloister walk is meant to evoke a fully redeemed Paradise, but tending the garden conjures up the sweat of Adam toiling the ground that resists his touch, cursed by thorns and thistles, rocks, serpents, and insects. And continually complaining people.

It is hard to live just outside the gates of Paradise. We expect to have now what we see inside that other garden. St. Paul said:

> Our citizenship is in heaven, and it is from there that we are expecting a Savior, the Lord Jesus Christ. He will transform the body of our humiliation that it may be conformed to the body of his glory, by the power that also enables him to make all things subject to himself. (Philippians 3:20-21)

Coping

We have citizenship, but we are not yet residents.

I had a friend in seminary who took this phrase from Paul seriously and announced whenever he could that he was a "citizen of heaven." Nobody minded much except when the seminarians traveled together, because at the Canadian border he would refuse to declare that he was from the United States. "Please don't say it!" they begged him.

"My citizenship is in heaven," he would say to the customs officials. Inevitably, the border police then pulled the students' car over for a few hours to search for drugs and contraband.

People of the early church expected the end of the world to occur at any time. The pending apocalypse did not stop them from arguing, apparently, but anticipating the kingdom of heaven breaking in on them at any moment did make the reality of heavenly citizenship vibrant in daily work. Living in two times in the same world broke time apart into signs and wonders for the apostles. Living in the end of time heightens the expectation of healing: a miracle is the healing of Paradise without the wait.

None is the hour of the Beautiful Gate. None anticipates the miraculous turning of sourness into sanctity, complaint into contemplation—perhaps even the wonder of healing.

> All the people saw him walking and praising God, and they recognized him as the one who used to sit and ask for alms at the Beautiful Gate of the temple; and they were filled with wonder and amazement at what had happened to him. (Acts 3:9-10)

These are the thoughts that help me through the ninth hour—these and a few prayers, the extraction of a few weeds, and a cup of tea with a little honey.

Finishing my tea, still on my knees in the garden, it is time to go back into the parish hall. But first—footsteps. I look up. A face, smiling. "Glad to see you," says the continually complaining person. "Nice day. The garden is coming along, isn't it?"

Amazing. A miracle.

Coping

> *Quench now on earth the flames of strife;*
> *from passion's heat preserve our life;*
> *and while you keep our body whole,*
> *pour healing peace upon our soul.*

Ambrose of Milan,
Hymn 21 in *The Hymnal 1982*

111

twelve

Magnifying

The Hour of Vespers

If I say, "Surely the darkness will
   cover me,
   and the light around me turn to night,"
Darkness is not dark to you;
the night is as bright as the day;
   darkness and light to you are both
   alike.

Psalm 139:10-11

N ot long ago I taught the story of Mary and her cousin Elizabeth to a group of little girls between the ages of five and nine. We read the traditional poetic phrases from the Bible:

> In the days of King Herod of Judea, there was a priest named Zechariah.... His wife was a descendant of Aaron, and her name was Elizabeth. Both of them were righteous before God, living blamelessly according to all the commandments and regulations of the Lord. But they had no children, because Elizabeth was barren, and both were getting on in years. (Luke 1:5-7)

The children already know a lot of things about the story. For instance, they know that Aaron the priest was Moses' brother and that he lived a long time before Jesus. The twelve jewels on Aaron's breastplate represent the twelve tribes of Israel, which he wore close to his heart like the slogans on a tee-shirt. The children can name the twelve tribes: if Elizabeth was a daughter of Aaron, she belonged to the Levites, the tribe of priests. The children also understand that the more they learn, the more there is to learn and every detail connects in some interesting way to something else in the Bible. And they know that angels almost always say, "Fear not!" because angels can be terrifying.

We read the text, and the children listen pretty carefully. But they are anxious to get to the part after they choose which characters they will be so that they can dress up and pretend. For some reason tonight they all want to be boys. So the part of Zechariah goes first, and Maggie's old Zechariah puts on his beard, robe, and prayer shawl, takes a staff, and totters off to the mosquito-net Holy of Holies.

> Once when he was serving as priest before God and his section was on duty, he was chosen by lot, according to the custom of the priesthood, to enter the sanctuary of the Lord and offer incense. Now at the time of the incense offering, the whole assembly of the people was praying outside. (Luke 1:8-10)

We would have let Maggie burn incense in the temple, but our basement room behind the Thrift Shop has poor ventilation.

Magnifying

Little Ashley, who wears pink dresses and lace and ribbons to church on Sunday, is disappointed that she cannot be Zechariah, but concedes that Gabriel can be as manly as she wants him to be. Reluctantly she dresses herself as an archangel— but an archangel with a sword, like St. Michael. Meanwhile Emma and Sarah busily stuff pillows into their women's robes. Sarah carries the baby John the Baptist so high that the pillows chafe her chin. But this annunciation will not take place on the road, in the manner of Renaissance painting, because Sarah's Elizabeth cannot even get out of her chair.

Gabriel, sword unsheathed, appears in the Holy of Holies to terrify Zechariah and let him know he will have John the Baptist for a son. He strikes Zechariah dumb, which is good because Maggie loves to pretend but does not like to make up the words. Now, in the fullness of time, Gabriel crosses the room to face Emma.

Knowing how terrifying angels can be, with or without swords, Emma shrieks and falls into a dead faint like a possum, paws in the air.

"Come on, Emma!" says Ashley. Emma, not moving, opens her eyes. "Okay... Mary! Fear not, you are going to have a baby!"

Emma looks through her paws at her bunched-up belly. "I can see that."

The rest of us angels have been holding our breath, waiting to hear what Mary will say. What if she says no? we wonder. Eventually she says yes, we breathe again, and Mary cooperates enough to take her trip from Galilee to the other side of the room near Jerusalem, where the over-stuffed Elizabeth waits helplessly in her chair like a bug on its back. When Mary begins her ecstatic canticle, we all say the *Magnificat* together. Then we play with magnifying glasses, wondering aloud about souls and prayer and how the Lord magnifies our souls.

My soul doth magnify the Lord, intensifying the sacred light within me like the horizon magnifying the full moon. In turn, my soul, like the rising moon, reflects God's light. *He that is mighty hath magnified me*—but I forget. The Almighty has done great things for me, but if I did not say these things at the hour of Vespers, I would be as

preoccupied with my own survival as a bat hunt-
ing mosquitoes when the sun goes down.

The church at Vespers reminds me of the beauty of the human soul. And even then, I might take
the words for granted except that Vespers is the
hour of incense, when Zechariah was struck
dumb by Gabriel for doubting, questioning the
wisdom of God. We sing the most beautiful
antiphons to introduce the *Magnificat,* and at the
moment we sing the Song of Mary, we replenish
the incense in the bowl—just when I need it most.

I need to know my soul magnifies the Lord
just then, because I find the evening a fearful time,
especially in winter when the light fades so early
and the time spent in darkness is so long. When I
was a little girl, I loved the warm and loving darkness, the moments after my mother turned out the
light and before I fell asleep. I never wanted or
needed a night light. But adulthood has made the
coming of darkness a fearful thing, and in winter
the early nightfall and long evenings try my soul
with unnamed fears.

The word "vesper" in Latin means evening,
from the Greek Hesperus, the evening star, Venus.
The church remembers the hour as the time of the

Incarnation, the Word becoming flesh. It remembers this hour as the time when Jesus, celebrating the Passover, broke bread and poured wine, instituting the eucharist with the words, *This is my body given for you; this is my blood, shed for you.* This is the hour of the body of Jesus, being born, living, given in thanksgiving in bread and wine. He carried the covenant in his body until his Passover. Vespers is also the hour of his body lifeless and caked with blood, taken down from the cross by his mother and his friends, washed, and anointed with oils and balm, herbs and spices, for burial.

Singing the *Magnificat* at Vespers, I see the just-pregnant Mary after she has walked a three-day journey from Galilee to the Judean hills near Jerusalem and entered the house of Elizabeth. Mary observes her cousin's body swollen with life on her aged frame. *When Elizabeth heard Mary's greeting, the child leaped in her womb* (Luke 1:41). And while Elizabeth's baby leaps in her womb, Mary suddenly "gets it." There Elizabeth lies upon her mat, probably overstuffed like Sarah, with swollen feet, ankles, and breasts, uncomfortable with excess body fluids, misfired hormones, small back pain, restricted bladder. And Mary sees herself in Elizabeth, later in her own pregnancy, sharing her body uncomfortably with an as yet unknown but intimate life.

Now it is real. Now I get it. Now I understand what that angel meant. Now I see the miracle of Incarnation. The Lord magnifies my soul so I can perceive this light I bear.

I see also what Mary does not yet see—*and a sword will pierce your own soul too* (Luke 2:35)—magnified more vividly than any halo proclaiming her holiness. I see Mary holding her son's dead body.

Two women, one carrying a child touched by the Holy Spirit who will baptize with water, another carrying the unborn Holy Spirit who will baptize with fire; two women carrying the light inside themselves in the time of darkness. The miracle is not the Incarnation of God through the working of the Holy Spirit; the miracle is the ordinary body, yours and mine, carrying this marvelous incarnate light.

At Vespers we sing an evening hymn, the *Phos hilaron,* and place incense into the bowl of glowing charcoal:

O gracious Light,
pure brightness of the everliving Father
   in heaven,
O Jesus Christ, holy and blessed!

120   Now as we come to the setting of the sun,
and our eyes behold the vesper light,
we sing your praises, O God: Father, Son,
   and Holy Spirit.

You are worthy at all times to be praised
   by happy voices,
O Son of God, O Giver of life,
and to be glorified through all the worlds.

At Vespers we burn our fear like a sin offering
in the bowl of incense. We burn our blindness, the
way we pretend we have never seen a miracle,
upon the altar of incense. We burn our frustra-
tions with the limitations of our bodies and
minds. We burn the dozens of daytime sins and
offer them as a fragrant sacrifice to the Dark Love
waiting for us behind our fear of the dark.

Magnifying

Almighty God, we give you thanks for sur-
rounding us, as daylight fades, with the
brightness of the vesper light; and we
implore you of your great mercy that, as
you enfold us with the radiance of this
light, so you would shine into our hearts
the brightness of your Holy Spirit; through
Jesus Christ our Lord. Amen.

121

prayer for light,
BCP 110

thirteen

Returning

The Hour of Compline

Lighten our darkness, we beseech thee, O Lord; and by thy great mercy defend us from all perils and dangers of this night; for the love of thy only Son, our Saviour, Jesus Christ. Amen.

collect for aid against perils
(1928 BCP)

I used to say this prayer kneeling at the side of my bed, my beautiful white prayer book in my hands. During my childhood, I was confident the Lord would protect me from the perils and dangers of the night. And, after all, my parents were downstairs, my father in the shaft of blue light cast by the television and my mother in the bright kitchen working on a project—perhaps a ship model or something else worth prowling down the stairs to glimpse before sneaking back up to bed.

But now I know the dangers of the night. For many years I was the sole parent locking up the house and putting out the lights, tucking in pajama-clad little bodies against the cold, singing the songs and telling the stories, administering the talisman kiss to ward off the dangers of the night and softly saying the prayer against its perils.

In this new phase of life with Bill and Patrick, saying the night prayers completes the day's sanctification of our home. Making this house into a place of prayer has been a slow but steady process. I still have blue roses on my wall between the ugly brown seams. But I love it when friends come to my house to "retreat" or when a monk

or nun finds our home "restful." Whole indus-
tries, journals, magazines, and showrooms are
devoted to home furnishing, remodeling, and dec-
orating. But prayer can also help make a house a
home—a work of art molded out of tragedy, dis-
appointment, sorrow and loss, joy, laughter,
learning and growing, beauty and balance, har-
mony and humor, and not least of all, surprise.
Prayer takes the material of life and signs our
soul's own signature in offering everything back
to God.

The neighborhood children play in the street
as long as they can in the evening, bicycling in cir-
cles, drawing pictures and hopscotch squares with
fat chalk onto the pavement; the teenagers play at
the basketball hoop under the streetlight in the
chilly darkness. One neighbor keeps an eye on
children and dogs alike, lest a foot or paw tread-
ing the narrow strip of grass should prompt him
to call the police. Their voices and the sound of
the highway over the bridge, the smell of marinara sauce and fermenting apples, offer a comforting familiarity as night falls.

In the early evening I tidy the house, straight-
ening the lace tablecloths, uncluttering the pile of

boots by the door, arranging tiny flowers in miniature vases, trying to make our space inviting, beautiful, and orderly. Bill cooks. He prepares meals effortlessly. When I cook, I fuss. I do not think I've really done my job unless I have parboiled something early in the day, sautéed onions and garlic, made a white sauce or gravy. Bill complains I spend too much money on ingredients. So we choose Bill's way. He bakes a fish to perfection in the toaster oven or outside on the grill. He makes imaginative salads out of anything the refrigerator might hold. The kitchen is his domain and the table mine. I love to set a beautiful table; I want to sit down and eat together. If it were left to Bill, we would eat standing up against the counter or in front of the television. So we choose my way.

When Lady's ears become puppy-huge I let her out and she runs down the street to meet Patrick, relating to him her day's adventures in woofs and sniffs and nudges with her nose. All the while she is decoding the events of Patrick's day through the jumble of smells on his shoes and clothes, backpack and jacket.

When friends ask if I am happy that we moved from the mountain to the village, I think of this moment of the day, when my son walks down the street to our house. "Are you happy you moved from the mountain?" they ask. This is the wrong question. I miss the beautiful view and the farmhouse, of course. Ask me instead how prayer can make a home a small paradise out of the kind of profound contentment that comes from the practice of gratitude—the sheer happy surprise of continually finding my way back home.

Once I met a woman who had been fighting with the Allied resistance in Norway during World War II. She was captured and tortured by the Nazis. The torturers, thinking she was dead, came to check her body. At that moment she had an experience of light, deep and comforting light, "as if my mother were home at the kitchen table with the light on, waiting for me," she recalled. At the Nuremberg trials my friend was sought out by one of the officers who had been ordered to torture her. He wanted to know about "the light" he had seen surrounding her—for which neither his ideology nor her pious upbringing had prepared them.

Returning

The time of day my son comes home may be the most important moment of my life. Having the porch light on; the smells of cooking; the order, balance, and refreshment of the house itself as he does his homework late into the night may secretly give him some sense that all we do is practice for some sacred moment. Perhaps someday in facing danger and death, a divine sign disguised in the symbol of home may save him.

Meanwhile, we conclude our day with the most mundane of evenings, each settled at our studious little stations, our three computers in the three rooms upstairs, and yet available to one another. "Do you have Kathy and Bob's phone number?" "How do you spell Thor Heyerdahl?" "How do I get these labels to print onto the envelope?" "Did Lady eat supper?" Downstairs, cable television is still a novelty in which we indulge too much. Bill and Patrick are both quiet men. Of our household trio I am the most effusive. This is a first for me—I have never lived in such a calm household.

Nevertheless, as evening draws toward night, I am more and more aware of another presence, even more quiet, within the house. No matter how busy or distracted or tired I am, familiar music begins winding round and round my mind. The music emerges from habit. I hear in my head the plainsong verses of Compline from the service music of the hymnal. When I don't respond, the music presses in on me until I find myself humming or singing.

128

Once the night dormitory prayers of monks, the prayers for Compline were brought into church worship by the fourth century, summing up the day and summing up life. *Grant us a peaceful night and a perfect end.* The sacred day is the sacred life. Going to sleep anticipates death, so we just say it without fuss—Compline is practice for dying. *Into your hands, O Lord, I commend my spirit,* the officiant chants. We respond, *For you have redeemed me, O Lord, O God of Truth.*

In some monastic houses where I stay, the monks process to the Lady altar after Compline to sing the *Salve Regina,* the hymn to Mary, Queen of Heaven. I do not say the *Salve* in my own prayers at home, but I love singing this with the monks when I visit in their homes. Sometimes I think singing the *Salve Regina* is like having the Queen of Heaven tucking you in for the night.

When she senses it is nearly time to get ready for sleep, Lady sneaks under our bed. For some reason she thinks sleeping under the bed is wrong and so she hardly breathes lest we find her. Our lights are out, but the streetlight shines brightly into the house. Traffic on the highway shrieks, and Bill turns on a fan for white noise to shut it out. Like his waking up, his going to sleep is untroubled.

Neither the Queen of Heaven in her starry diadem, nor the image of light shining in the darkness, soothes me to sleep. For me, the divine presence comes through the symbol of wings.

> He who dwells in the shelter of the Most
>   High abides under the shadow of the
>   Almighty....
> He shall cover you with his pinions, and
>   you shall find refuge under his wings....
> Because you have made the LORD your
>   refuge, and the Most High your
>   habitation.
>
>   (Psalm 91:1, 4, 9)

Behind the lights and the darkness, in the silence behind the chanted ancient words, wings wait to take me toward the home that I have longed for since I was born. We are created for reverence, and in this worship of love unseen, I sense six-winged seraphs, incomprehensible in their multiple dimensions, folding and unfolding in and out of human consciousness. And so I chant, *Keep me as the apple of your eye; hide me under the shadow of your wings* (Psalm 17:8). When I die you will carry my prayer within your wings into the holy darkness, my dust falling to earth and back to stars, the sanctity that has mingled with my body censing the dust I leave behind.

Lady, gently snoring under the bed, waits for me to rise, so that she may nudge me toward another day.

Everlasting God, you have ordained and constituted in a wonderful order the ministries of angels and mortals: Mercifully grant that, as your holy angels always serve and worship you in heaven, so by your appointment they may help and defend us here on earth; through Jesus Christ our Lord, who lives and reigns with you and the Holy Spirit, one God, for ever and ever. Amen.

collect of the holy angels,
BCP 251

Cowley Publications is a ministry of the Society of St. John the Evangelist, a religious community for men in the Episcopal Church. Emerging from the Society's tradition of prayer, theological reflection, and diversity of mission, the press is centered in the rich heritage of the Anglican Communion.

Cowley Publications seeks to provide books, audio cassettes, and other resources for the ongoing theological exploration and spiritual development of the Episcopal Church and others in the body of Christ. To this end, it is dedicated to developing a new generation of theological writers, encouraging them to produce timely, creative, and stimulating publications of excellence, and making these publications available widely, reaching both clergy and lay persons.